CAROLYN BEAR

Illustrated by John Prater

OXFORD
UNIVERSITY PRESS

OXFORD
UNIVERSITY PRESS

Great Clarendon Street, Oxford OX2 6DP

Oxford University Press is a department of the University of Oxford.
It furthers the University's objective of excellence in research, scholarship,
and education by publishing worldwide in

Oxford   New York

Auckland   Cape Town   Dar es Salaam   Hong Kong   Karachi
Kuala Lumpur   Madrid   Melbourne   Mexico City   Nairobi
New Delhi   Shanghai   Taipei   Toronto

With offices in

Argentina   Austria   Brazil   Chile   Czech Republic   France   Greece
Guatemala   Hungary   Italy   Japan   Poland   Portugal   Singapore
South Korea   Switzerland   Thailand   Turkey   Ukraine   Vietnam

Oxford is a registered trade mark of Oxford University Press
in the UK and in certain other countries

Text © Carolyn Bear 1999

The moral rights of the author have been asserted

Database right Oxford University Press (maker)

First published 1999
This edition 2005

British Library Cataloguing in Publication Data
Data available

ISBN: 978-0-19-919987-7

9 10 8

Available in packs
Stage 12 More Stories B Pack of 6: ISBN: 978-0-19-919981-5

Stage 12 More Stories B Class Pack: ISBN: 978-0-19-919988-4

Guided Reading Cards also available: ISBN: 978-0-19-919990-7

Cover artwork by Martin Cottam

Printed in Malaysia by
MunSang Printers Sdn Bhd

Paper used in the production of this book is a natural,
recyclable product made from wood grown in sustainable forests.
The manufacturing process conforms to the environmental
regulations of the country of origin.

Chapter One

Scrapman wasn't an ordinary man. He was a mechanical man. In fact, he was the most incredible mechanical man that had ever been made.

He had arms that could reach twice as far as an ordinary man. He had telescopic legs that could stretch out as long as stilts when he wanted to reach something high up.

But he didn't have a very good brain.

You see, Scrapman belonged to the owner of a scrap-yard. His name was Winston. Winston used to collect the useful bits from all the old worn-out things people sent to his scrap-yard.

He'd made Scrapman out of loads of different parts. His brain was made from a personal-organizer that had been thrown away because it was always going wrong. And it still went wrong. But now Scrapman went wrong with it.

Like this morning ...

'Od ear,' said Scrapman as he put his head out of the window to see what the weather was like – he'd forgotten to open it first!

Winston was just arriving for work. He put down his bag of sandwiches and stood with his hands on his hips.

'Scrapman! How many times have I told you to think before you do something!'

'Volly solly,' said Scrapman. (You see, it wasn't a very good brain at all.)

Winston was very quiet all through that day. He hardly whistled at all as he worked which was a *bad* sign.

Scrapman felt very ashamed of himself.

As he worked in the scrap-yard, he thought very carefully before he did anything. He thought before he lifted anything up and he thought before he put it down again.

In fact, he thought so much that hardly anything got done that day.

At last, Winston had mended the
window, eaten his sandwiches,
finished his work, and gone home
for the night.

Scrapman sat down inside the shed
feeling very sad. How he would love to
be clever like Winston.

Right now, whenever he had any
spare time, Winston was working on
this fantastic invention. It was huge.
It took up almost half the space in the
shed and there were blueprints for it
pinned all over the walls. It was a
wonderful aeroplane that didn't need
petrol to make it fly.

Scrapman sat on the floor and stared at the invention. It was boring being on his own in the shed at night. He didn't have anything to do.

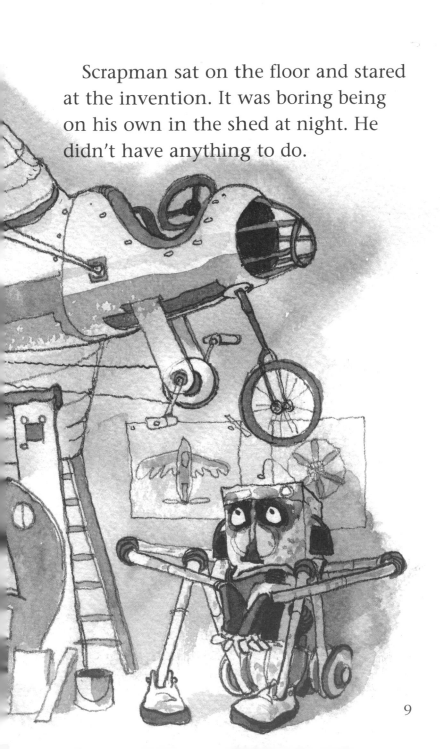

He stood up and pulled faces at himself in the shiny new glass window.

Then he sat down again and played noughts and crosses with himself in the dust on the floor. And, as usual, he lost.

Then he picked up Winston's screwdriver. There was a pile of bits and pieces on the workbench. There were some nuts and bolts and screws.

There were some pieces of wire, and some little triangles of metal that had been cut off the corners of something else. There was also an odd-shaped cone that looked a bit like a nose.

Scrapman started to fiddle with the pieces, putting them together and taking them apart again. And then all of a sudden, he could hardly believe his eyes. He'd made something!

Scrapman looked at it and it looked back at Scrapman. It had two pointed ears and a nose and whiskers. In fact it looked just like a ...

'SCRAPCAT!' said Scrapman.

He was very excited. If he worked a little longer he would have someone to share the shed with. Someone to play with through the long, lonely nights when Winston wasn't there.

He worked like a madman all
through the night.

He found a big, fat tin for a body
and fixed the head to it.

Then he cut four legs off a chair and
stuck those underneath, and he found
just the thing for a tail!

As the sun rose, Scrapman stood
back and admired his brilliant piece
of work.

'Pertty pussy,' he called. But Scrapcat
didn't move.

Scrapman got a length of string and
pulled it across the floor – but still
nothing happened.

'Od ear,' said Scrapman. He'd made a Scrapcat but something was wrong.

All the cats he'd seen in the scrap-yard could stand up and sit down, and walk along walls and jump on to the roof. But this cat didn't do anything at all.

Sadly, he picked up Scrapcat and hid him away in a cupboard.

Chapter Two

The next morning, Winston arrived at the scrap-yard to find Scrapman fast asleep.

'Get up my lad. There's work to be done,' he said briskly. 'Today's the day I'm going to finish my great invention.'

'O volly good,' said Scrapman.

Winston put on his overall and turned on his radio. Then he picked up his screwdriver and went to his workbench.

'That's odd,' he said.

He looked under the table for all the things he'd left out on the top.

Then he caught sight of his chair. He turned it upside down to see what had happened to the legs.

'That's very odd indeed,' said Winston.

Scrapman didn't say anything. He stood in front of the cupboard.

'Scrapman,' said Winston. 'Did
you see anybody come into the shed
last night?'

Scrapman shook his head. 'No body,'
he said.

So Winston went off to the far side
of the scrap-yard to search for some
more nuts and bolts and wire, and
another cone that looked like a nose.

Scrapcat put his head on one side and looked at Scrapman. He stared at him for quite some time.

Then he stood up on his back paws and walked over to Scrapman – just like a human being.

'Oh no,' said Scrapman. 'You are not a hu mung bean. You are a cat.'

But Scrapcat didn't understand.

'Look,' said Scrapman, getting down on all fours. 'Copy me. This is how a cat is meant to walk.'

Scrapcat got down on all fours. But when Scrapman stood up again, so did Scrapcat.

'Od ear,' said Scrapman, and he got down on all fours again.

That's when Emma arrived. Emma was Scrapman's special friend. She came every week to teach him how to speak properly.

'It's not *od ear*, Scrapman. It's *oh dear*,' said Emma. 'What are you doing on the floor?'

Scrapman sat down on a chair. And
Scrapcat sat down on a stool beside
him and crossed his legs.

'What a funny cat,' said Emma. 'I've
never seen a cat sit like that before.'

'He thinks he's a hu mung bean,'
said Scrapman sadly. 'You see – he's
never seen a real cat.'

'Oh, poor Scrapcat,' said Emma. And she ran all the way home and came back with her own cat – Patch.

'Now this is a real cat,' said Emma.

Patch took one look at Scrapcat and all his fur stood on end. Scrapcat did his best to copy him. Then Patch's tail fluffed out like a bottle-brush. Which wasn't a problem for Scrapcat.

Patch stood on the tips of all his toes and he hissed. Then he shot out through the door as fast as his legs would carry him.

And Scrapcat raced out after him.

'Od ear,' said Scrapman. And he and Emma ran after the cats as fast as they could.

They searched the streets for hours and hours. Then they heard a sad sound coming from above:

'*Miaow ... miaow ... miaow.*'

It was Patch. He was stuck right at the top of a tall tree.

'Oh dear, he can't get down,' said Emma.

But this wasn't a problem for Scrapman. He just stretched his telescopic legs to their full length and lifted him down.

Scrapman gave Patch back to Emma. Then they looked for Scrapcat.

They called and whistled and banged
a fork on a plate, but they couldn't
find Scrapcat anywhere.

So, very sadly, Scrapman went back
to the scrap-yard without him.

While Scrapman was out, Winston
had come back with some nuts and
bolts and pieces of wire. But he
couldn't find another cone that looked
like a nose.

All the same, he put on his overalls
and went to his workbench and
turned on the radio. But
nothing happened.

'How very odd,' thought Winston. He'd put in some new batteries only the day before.

When Scrapman came back Winston looked at him sternly.

'Scrapman. Do you know where the batteries from my radio have gone?'

Scrapman shook his head sadly. If he'd known where the batteries had gone, he'd have known where Scrapcat was. But Scrapcat was lost.

Chapter Three

That night Scrapman sat alone in the shed feeling lonelier than ever.

He stared out of the new glass window but he couldn't see Scrapcat anywhere. This was not surprising because Scrapcat was sitting outside the door waiting to be let in.

Scrapman tossed and turned but he couldn't sleep. At last, he decided to go out to have another look for Scrapcat. As he went out of the door, he tripped over something.

It was Scrapcat.

That's when Scrapman realized that something else was wrong. Scrapcat didn't miaow. He couldn't miaow because Scrapman hadn't thought of giving him a voice to miaow with.

Scrapman scratched his head and racked his brain. He stared out at the scrap-yard where all the old broken machines and cars were glinting in the moonlight.

Then he had an idea.

He took Winston's screwdriver and climbed into the driver's seat of one of the cars. He was very busy in there for quite some time.

The next morning, Winston came into the scrap-yard with a newspaper in his hand.

'Just look at that,' he said to Scrapman. He pointed to where it said, 'Beware – Burglars in Town!'

'Od ear,' said Scrapman.

'That explains it,' said Winston. 'First it was the parts for my great invention. Then it was the legs from my chair. And after that it was the batteries from my radio. What will be next?'

Scrapman stood in front of the cupboard and said: 'I dun no.'

'My great invention!' said Winston. 'That's what it will be. We can't be too careful.'

And he got busy fixing an old burglar alarm he'd found in a skip, on to the wall. When he'd finished, he tested it to see if it worked. It did.

It went, '*Brrr…rrrrrrrr…rrrrrrrrr,*' very loudly indeed.

That evening, when Winston had gone home, Emma arrived with Patch. Scrapman let Scrapcat out of the cupboard.

Patch took one look at Scrapcat and arched his back and hissed. He miaowed very loudly.

And Scrapcat arched his back and went, '*Honk, honk*'.

Patch looked at Scrapcat in disgust. He looked at Scrapcat as if he was the most stupid cat on this planet.

'You silly thing, Scrapman,' said Emma. 'That's not the kind of noise a cat makes.'

'Od ear,' said Scrapman sadly. And he bent down and stroked Scrapcat so that his feelings wouldn't be hurt.

Then Emma bent down and stroked
Patch so that he wouldn't feel left out.
And Patch rolled on his back and
purred loudly.

'You see, that's the kind of noise a
cat makes,' said Emma.

'Honk, honk,' said Scrapcat.

'Od ear,' said Scrapman.

When Emma had gone, Scrapman
sat with Scrapcat and felt very sad. He
had made a cat. But it wasn't a very
good cat. Scrapcat couldn't miaow.
Scrapcat couldn't even purr.

He sat for a long time staring at the
wall and then he had an idea.

He took Winston's screwdriver and stretched up to his full height and took down the burglar alarm. He was busy with it for quite some time.

He took Scrapcat apart and screwed in the bell he'd taken from inside the burglar alarm, and he put him back together again. Then he tested him to see if it worked.

Scrapcat rolled on his back and went: *'Brrrrrr…brrrrrrrrr… brrrrrrrrr.'*

'Oh volly good,' said Scrapman. It was a much better purr than Patch had. It was the loudest purr any cat had ever had.

The next time Emma and Patch
came to visit Scrapman, he took
Scrapcat out of the cupboard and
Scrapcat rolled on his back and purred.
'Brrrrrr…brrrrrrrrr…brrrrrrrrr.'

Patch jumped out of the window.
Emma stood with her hands over her
ears and shouted at Scrapman.

'What a terrible noise. Stop him!'

'Od ear,' said Scrapman.

Scrapcat couldn't miaow properly.
He couldn't even purr properly.
Clearly, he was a hopeless cat.

When Emma had gone, Scrapman picked up Winston's screwdriver.

You see, he had decided to take Scrapcat apart and give back the bell from the alarm, and the batteries from the radio, and the legs from the chair, and the cone that looked a bit like a nose.

But Scrapman looked at Scrapcat.
And Scrapcat put his head on one side
and looked at Scrapman.

And Scrapman decided that it
wouldn't hurt to keep Scrapcat for just
one more night. He'd take him apart
in the morning.

So he put Scrapcat back in the
cupboard and went to sleep.

A little while later, two faces
appeared at the window. They were
staring at Winston's great invention.
They were BURGLARS!

In less than a minute they had
broken the window and climbed
inside. Because, of course, the burglar
alarm didn't go off, did it?

Before Scrapman even had time to wake up, they tied him up with a rope. Then they tied a dirty oily rag round Scrapman's mouth so that he couldn't shout. And then they started to drag Winston's great invention out of the shed.

Scrapman looked on helplessly. He couldn't do anything.

But Scrapcat heard the noise the burglars made. He jumped out of the cupboard. He saw Scrapman tied up and he felt very sorry for him. So he went over and rubbed himself up against Scrapman.

That's when he started to purr. *'Brrrrrrr…brrrrrrrr…brrrrrrrrrrr.'*

Instantly, the burglars let go of the great invention and ran out of the shed. But they didn't get very far because someone had heard Scrapcat and telephoned the police.

Three police cars drove up just in time to catch the burglars as they were escaping in their van.

Soon Winston arrived. He untied
Scrapman and took off the oily rag,
and then he saw Scrapcat.

'Where did he come from?' he asked.

Scrapman hung his head. 'Out of the
cupboard,' he said.

Winston looked at Scrapcat carefully.
He looked at his ears and his whiskers
and his four wooden legs. He looked at
his nose that looked a bit like a cone.

He scratched his chin. Then he asked,
'Who made this cat, Scrapman?'

Scrapman felt very ashamed.
'Scrapman,' he said.

He waited for Winston to get very angry. But instead Winston put a hand on his shoulder and said, 'Scrapman, I had no idea you were so clever. He's a brilliant cat! He's the most wonderful cat I've ever seen! Do you realize we're the only scrap-yard in the whole world to have our very own guard cat?'

Scrapman couldn't believe that anyone could say anything so nice about him. What did it matter if he didn't have a very good brain? It worked, didn't it? And Scrapcat rolled on his back and purred.

'*Brrrrrrr...rrrrrrrrr...rrrrrrrrrr.*'

About the author

The idea for writing
this book came from a
whole load of letters I
was sent by the children
of Mapplewells School.
They wrote to tell me how
much they enjoyed the first book
about Scrapman, and several asked me
to write another book about him.

All their letters had fantastic
drawings on them, and there, right at
the top of a drawing by a boy called
Rory Miller, was something that looked
very much like … Scrapcat!

So Scrapman and I would like to
thank you, Rory, for inspiring the idea!